CW00434226

SAY MY NAME

Published in 2024 by OH!
An Imprint of Welbeck Non-Fiction Limited,
part of Welbeck Publishing Group.
Offices in: London – 20 Mortimer Street, London W1T 3JW
and Sydney – Level 17, 207 Kent St, Sydney NSW 2000 Australia
www.welbeckpublishing.com

Compilation text © Welbeck Non-Fiction Limited 2024
Design © Welbeck Non-Fiction Limited 2024

ISBN 978-1-80069-579-5

Compiled and written by: Malcolm Croft
Editorial: Victoria Denne
Project manager: Russell Porter
Production: Marion Storz

A CIP catalogue record for this book is available from the British Library

Printed in Dubai

10 9 8 7 6 5 4 3 2 1

SAY MY NAME

THE LITTLE GUIDE TO
BREAKING BAD

UNOFFICIAL AND UNAUTHORIZED

CONTENTS

INTRODUCTION

Let's begin in the only way a *Breaking Bad* book could, with the infinitely inspiring wit of the world's best blue-sky thinker, Jesse Pinkman…

Yo, Bitch!

Yes, welcome to the slow-burn, flask-filled world of *Breaking Bad*, without a doubt one of the purest and most addictive TV shows ever to come to a rolling boil on a Bunsen burner in front of our glazed-over eyeballs.

When the show first aired on U.S. network AMC on January 20, 2008 – fifteen years ago – nobody assumed it would be a ratings hit. And it wasn't; not at first. But eventually, it came to define, elevate and validate a new golden age of television – the streaming era. The fact that the show was unlike anything anyone had ever seen before as well was just a happy accident. Much like most of Walt and Jesse's misadventures.

During its five-season run, *Breaking Bad* broke the zeitgeist on several occasions, becoming the OG of bingewatchabilty when it transferred after two seasons to Netflix in 2010. Soon, popular culture's best watercooler conversations were of Walt and Jesse's transformation from good to bad (and back again); an unrelenting gift that kept on giving. Vince Gilligan, the creator, had given his audience a show as moreish as Walt's blue sky.

When its critically acclaimed final episode aired in 2013, and the dust of the Tohajiilee Desert settled and all the bad (and good) guys were dead, *Breaking Bad* had evolved into the stuff of legend, just like Heisenberg. TV has not been the same since.

To celebrate the enduring legacy of this ground-breaking game-changer, this tiny tome takes a trip down memory lane to reminisce about the time when Walt, Jesse, Skyler, Saul, Gus, Tuco, Mike and Hank all went a little too loco down in New Mexico, revealed via the writer's wealth of wicked wit and wisdom and classic, killer catchphrases now buried snugly in the tighty-whities of popular culture.

Be warned: don't binge all the book at once, read *lightly* (to paraphrase Walt) – we wouldn't want you to get hooked on the show all over again. Or would we?

Wanna cook?

CHAPTER

1

BIOLOGY

As we learn throughout all the bad and bastardly behaviour of Walter White during the show's run, nothing is more important to our cancer-contaminated chemistry teacher than biology. His family comes first no matter what.

However, Walt has three families, doesn't he? The biological one under his roof, the criminal one under his thumb and the cartel he's constantly trying to compound.

Let's bung the three together in a boiling flask and watch them bubble…

My name is Walter Hartwell White. I live at 308 Negra Arroyo Lane, Albuquerque, New Mexico, 87104. To all law enforcement entities, this is not an admission of guilt… Skyler, you are the love of my life. I hope you know that. Walter Junior, you're my big man. There are… there are going to be some things that you'll come to learn about me in the next few days. I just want you to know that no matter how it may look, I only had you in my heart. Goodbye.

Walt introduces himself as a family man without admitting to any criminal behaviour*, "Pilot", Season 1.

* See next page.

My name is Walter Hartwell White. I live at 308 Negra Arroyo Lane, Albuquerque, New Mexico, 87104. This is my confession. If you're watching this tape, I'm probably dead — murdered by my brother-in-law, Hank Schrader. Hank has been building a meth empire for over a year now and using me as his chemist.

Walt double-crosses Hank in a taped confession that mirrors the pilot episode, "Confessions", Season 5.

Someone has to protect this family from the man who protects this family.

Skyler, hitting the nail right on the head, "Cornered", Season 4.

Breaking & Entering 1

In 2022, *Breaking Bad* was voted the most binge-worthy TV boxset of all time, according to One Poll research.

The average "binge" of the show on Netflix lasts FIVE hours — in one sitting!

Skyler, all that I've done, all the sacrifices that I've made for this family, all of it will be for nothing if you don't accept what I've earned.

Walt tries to convince Skyler of his well-intentioned sacrifices in his shocking admission of guilt, "I.F.T.", Season 3.

Don't get me wrong. I think it's just great that Walt's back and he's feeling better. I just, I mean, he was… naked. He was *naked* in a supermarket. It wasn't Whole Foods, was it?

Marie, reliving Walt's supposed nude fugue state, "Bit By a Dead Bee", Season 2.

Breaking & Entering 2

When Jesse Pinkman escaped in a 1978 Chevy El Camino at the conclusion of the fifth season of *Breaking Bad,* his story was the only future left to write. *El Camino: A Breaking Bad Movie* was a huge hit, watched by 25,753,392 households in its first seven days, according to Netflix. Jesse's story was now complete.

How do you look bad exactly? Where is the 'I slept with my boss' bullet point? Because I can't seem to find that anywhere.*

Walt reminds Skyler that she's no angel in their situation, "Bullet Points", Season 4.

To which Skyler retorts, "For a fired schoolteacher who cooks crystal meth, I say you're coming out pretty much ahead."

I was at home watching TV. Some nature program about elephants… and Skyler and Holly were in another room.
I can hear them on the baby monitor. She was singing a lullaby. Oh, if I had just lived right up to that moment… and not one second more… that would have been perfect.

Walt confesses the day he wished was his last, "Fly", Season 3.

Your scumbag brother-in-law is finished.
Done. You understand? He'll be scrubbing
toilets in Tijuana for pennies and I'll be
standing over him to get my cut. I will
haunt his crusty ass forever until the day
he sticks a gun up his mouth and pulls
the trigger just to get me out of his head.
That's what happens next.

Jesse, to Walt, on Hank learning of his role in the cook,
"Sunset", Season 3.

Breaking & Entering

3

Walt and Jesse's signature Big Blue crystal meth is, for legal purposes, just blue ice rock candy crushed into pieces. The show's prop department originally approached the Candy Lady, a boutique sweet shop in Albuquerque owned by Debbie Ball, to produce an edible show prop for the first season that did not look like actual street meth.

The candy can now be bought in 100 g bags, complete with a note for law enforcement, should you be pulled over by police.

When you have children, you always have family. They will always be your priority, your responsibility, and a man provides. And he does it even when he's not appreciated or respected or even loved. He simply bears up and he does it. Because he's a man, Walter.

Gus lectures Walt about the importance of biology, "Green Light", Season 3.

You're the only thing that stands between him and an axe to the head.

Mike, to Jesse, on the future of Walt's life, "Green Light", Season 3.

Breaking Bad:
By the Numbers #1

54

The number of times
Jesse Pinkman ends a sentence
with the word "bitch" throughout
the show's 62 episodes.

Breaking & Entering 4

"We get a lot of credit for this detail-rich, very faithful unto itself sort of storytelling shape for the entire run of episodes. It's because we would be very careful to mine past episodes and hew to them faithfully in terms of plot details, and therefore make the whole thing feel like it was of a piece. We were looking backward not forward half the time, in other words."

Vince Gilligan, on the show's intricate plotting and detail, interview with Matt Edwards, *Den of Geek*, September 3, 2018.

You can screw Ted, you can screw the butcher, the mailman, whoever you want! Screw all! I'm not going anywhere.

Walt isn't afraid of Skyler's bed-buddy and boss, Ted Beneke, "Green Light", Season 3.

My children are blameless victims of their monstrous father, a man who you once knew quite well. Call it a beau geste. Call it liberal guilt. Call it whatever you want but do it.

Walt, to Elliott and Gretchen, after ensuring his children are financially protected for the rest of their lives, "Felina", Season 5.

Will you just… just leave us alone? You asshole.
Why are you still alive?
Why don't you just die already?
Just die.

Walter Junior admonishes Walt, upon learning the extent of his father's crimes, "Granite State", Season 5.

I'll give myself up if you promise me one thing: you keep the money. Never speak of it, never give it up. You pass it on to our children, give them everything. Will you do that? Please? Please, don't let me have done all this for nothing.

Walt makes promises with Skyler over the phone following her deal with Hank, "Buried", Season 5.

I can't go to the police, I can't stop laundering your money, I can't keep you out of this house, I can't even keep you out of my bed. All I can do is wait. That's it, that's the only good option. Hold on. Bide my time. And wait… For the cancer to come back.

Skyler outlines her hostage situation to her husband, "Fifty-One", Season 5.

Okay. So you took it upon yourself to give away $622,000 of my money to a man who had been sleeping with my wife.

Walt, to Saul, about Ted, "Live Free or Die", Season 5.

All I know is when he tells me that your employer took him out threatening to murder his family, I take notice. Because after all, what am I, if not family?

Saul tries to wriggle into Walt and Jesse's extended family, "End Times", Season 4.

I will kill your wife. I will kill your son. I will kill your infant daughter.

Gus tells Walt to leave the superlab (without Jesse, or his formula) – or else, "Crawl Space", Season 4.

If I had to put it in a word, I'd guess loyalty. Only maybe you got it for the wrong guy.

Mike questions Jesse's loyalty to either Gus or Walt, "Problem Dog", Season 4.

I have spent my whole life scared, frightened of things that could happen, might happen, might not happen. Fifty years I spent like that. Finding myself awake at three in the morning. But you know what? Ever since my diagnosis, I sleep just fine.

Walt begins to wake up from reality to confront his fears, "Better Call Saul", Season 2.

Jesse, look at me, you are a blow fish. Small in stature, not swift, not cunning, easy prey for predators. But the blow fish has a secret weapon, doesn't he? The blow fish puffs himself up five times larger than normal, but why?
Because it makes him intimidating, that's why. Intimidating so that the other scarier fish are scared off, and that's you. You are a blow fish. Don't you see? It's just all an illusion.
It's nothing but air.

Walt attempts to bolster Jesse's confidence with nothing but hot air, "Peekaboo", Season 2.

* Jesse later exclaims, "I'm blowfishin' it up!"

Doctor, my wife is seven months pregnant with a baby we didn't intend. My fifteen-year-old son has cerebral palsy. I am an extremely overqualified high school chemistry teacher. When I can work, I make $43,700 per year. I have watched all of my colleagues and friends surpass me in every way imaginable, and within eighteen months, I will be dead. And you ask why I ran?

Walt expositions to the doctor the plot, and why he faked his fugue state, "Bit By a Dead Bee", Season 2.

I need support. Me, the almost forty-year-old pregnant woman with the surprise baby on the way. And the husband with lung cancer who disappears for hours on end and I don't know where he goes and he barely even speaks to me anymore.

Skyler, to Hank, ridiculing Marie's "problems" in relation to her own, "Seven-Thirty-Seven", Season 2.

So you must be Daddy. Let me get this straight: I steal your dope, I beat the piss out of your mule boy, and then you walk in here, and you bring me more meth?! Woo! That's a brilliant plan, ese.

Tuco introduces himself to Walt, after extinguishing a cigarette on his tongue first, "Crazy Handful of Nothin", Season 1.

Breaking & Entering

"We wanted the viewers to watch closely and pay strict attention. And why would they do that unless they're being rewarded with internal logical consistency and with these little Easter eggs, these little details that if you watch closely, you get rewarded for?"

Vince Gilligan, on rewarding the audience, interview with Matt Edwards, *Den of Geek*, September 3, 2018.

I haven't been myself lately, but I love you. Nothing about that has changed, nothing ever will. So right now, what I need is for you to climb down out of my ass. Can you do that? Will you do that for me, honey? Will you please, just once, get off my ass, you know? I'd appreciate it, I really would.

Walt, to Skyler, requesting space as he transitions from chemistry teacher to meth manufacturer, "Cat's in the Bag", Season 1.

Jesse, you asked me if I was in the meth business or the money business. Neither. I'm in the empire business.*

Walt tells Jesse his long-term goals, "Dead Freight", Season 5.

*To which Jesse retorts, "Is a meth empire really something to be that proud of?"

CHAPTER

2

CHEMISTRY

Chemistry is at the heart of *Breaking Bad*. From ionic and covalent bonds (opposites attract, effectively) to complex compounds, ricin bean reactions to Walt's cancerous cells and, of course, the now-iconic chemistry onscreen between the actors.

We reveal now the dynamic, kinetic energy at the core of the characters' relationships with each other and the drug tyrant that mixes all the chemicals together — Heisenberg.

The soul? There's nothing but chemistry here.

Walt speaks to Gretchen in a flashback while calculating the chemistry that makes people human, "… And the Bag's in the River", Season 1.

I simply respect the chemistry. The chemistry must be respected.

Walt, to Gus, about the argued "overweening" pride he feels for his meth formula, "Green Light", Season 3.

Well, technically, chemistry is the study of matter. But I prefer to see it as the study of change.

Walt foreshadows his transformation via metaphor, "Pilot", Season 1.

Breaking & Entering

6

"Redemption is in the eye of the viewer. We didn't set out to damn or redeem anyone. I don't think there's any redemption for Walter White, but that doesn't mean he has to go out in a sulphurous cloud of ignominy. It remains to be seen if he goes out standing on his feet or lying on his back."

Vince Gilligan, on Walt's legacy being in the hands of the viewer not the show's writers, interview with Martin Miller, *LA Times*, September 27, 2013.

This ain't chemistry. This is art. Cooking is art. And the shit I cook is the bomb. Chili P is my signature, man!

Jesse reacts negatively to Walt's accusations about his Chili P recipe, "Pilot", Season 1.

The shit you cook is shit. I saw your set-up. Ridiculous. You and I will not make garbage. We will produce a chemically pure and stable product that performs as advertised. No adulterants. No baby formula. No chili powder.

Walt's quest for meth perfection subverts his own crumbling stability and purity, "Pilot", Season 1.

We make poison for people who don't care. We probably have the most unpicky customers in the world.

Jesse shows a lack of basic customer service, "Fly", Season 3.

We got new players in town. We don't know who they are, where they come from, but they possess an extremely high skill set. Me personally? I'm thinking Albuquerque just might have a new kingpin.

Hank, to Gomez, on ABQ's new meth maestro, "Cancer Man", Season 1.

Breaking & Entering 7

"Bryan Cranston said being Walter White was like wearing a very heavy overcoat. The good news for him is he would take off the overcoat at the weekends and he would go back to being Bryan. I'm glad for him in that sense. I feel like Walter White was in my head 24 hours a day."

Vince Gilligan, on Walter White, interview with Jacob Stolworthy, *Independent*, March 23, 2018.

To hell with your cancer. I've been living with cancer for the better part of a year. Right from the start, it's a death sentence. That's what they keep telling me. Well, guess what? Every life comes with a death sentence.

Walt, on his growing frustration at his ongoing cancer treatment, "Hermanos", Season 4.

Breaking Bad: By the Numbers #2

62

The number of episodes in *Breaking Bad*'s five-series run is deliberate. The 62nd element on the periodic table is Samarium, a rare earth metal that can be used to treat a range of cancers, including Walt's lung cancer.

Yeah, Mr White!
Yeah, science!

Jesse responds positively to Walt's plan to cook
more, "A No-Rough-Stuff-Type Deal", Season 1.

You cook, I sell. That was the division of labor when we started all this. And that's exactly how we should have kept it! 'Cause I sure as hell didn't find myself locked in a trunk or on my knees with a gun to my head before your greedy old ass came along, alright?

Jesse tells Walt how it really is once the power dynamic shifts, "Breakage", Season 2.

Never give up control. Live life on your own terms.

Walt dismisses a fellow cancer patient's bumbling life philosophy, "Hermanos", Season 4.

Smoking marijuana, eating
Cheetos and masturbating
do not constitute plans in
my book.

Walt ridicules Jesse for his inability to make plans,
"4 Days Out", Season 2.

Clear the contaminant?! We're making meth here, alright? Not space shuttles!

Jesse gets heated over Walt's safety and sanity protocols following the arrival of the fly, "Fly", Season 3.

The universe is random; it's not inevitable, it's simple chaos. It's subatomic particles and endless pings, collision — that's what science teaches us.

Walt, against all odds, has a random drink with Jane's dad after her death, "Fly", Season 3.

Breaking & Entering

"When I first read the script, I thought, Tony Soprano, Dexter, Vic Mackey. When we were introduced to them, they were already that kind of person. But I'm not sure this has happened before: where we take one kind of person – bright, depressed, just turned 50, dying of cancer – and say, 'For the next two years, he's going to go on the greatest roller-coaster ride of his life.'"

Bryan Cranston, on Walter White, interview with Brett Martin, *GQ*, July 15, 2013.

Gale Boetticher was a good man and a
good chemist and I cared about him.
He didn't deserve what happened
to him. But I'd shoot him again and
tomorrow and the next day and the day
after that. When you make it Gale versus
me, or Gale versus Jesse, Gale loses!
Simple as that.

Walt, to Gus, explaining his logic behind Gale's murder,
"Box Cutter", Season 4.

Well? Get back to work.

Gus, after slicing Victor's throat, gives Walt what he asked for, "Box Cutter", Season 4.

This is what comes of blood for blood, Hector. Sangre por sangre.

Gus updates Hector Salamanca on the deaths of his nephews, "Hermanos", Season 4.

Sometimes I feel like I never actually make any of my own. Choices, I mean. My entire life, it just seems I never… you know, had a real say about any of it. Now this last one, cancer… all I have left is how I choose to approach this.

Walt discussing his choices about how to approach his cancer diagnosis, "Gray Matter", Season 1.

It's kind of funny. When I got my diagnosis – cancer – I said to myself, 'Why me?' And then, the other day when I got the good news, I said the same thing.

Walt lets his macabre mask slip a little in a speech at a party, "Over", Season 2.

Breaking & Entering

"I was talking to a buddy of mine. Both of us had been unemployed for a while, and we were wondering what to do next. Either he or I joked about putting a crystal meth lab in the back of an RV and driving around the country cooking meth and making money. As we were talking, the idea for this character just kind of popped into my head. It was that proverbial lightning strike."

Vince Gilligan, on the ideation of *Breaking Bad*, interview with Scott Myers, *Medium*, May 8, 2010.

I was told that the man I'd be meeting with was very careful. A cautious man. I believe we are alike in that way. If you are who I think you are, you should give me another chance.

Walt meets his business partner, Gus Fring, for the first time at Los Pollos Hermanos, "Mandala", Season 2.

You're really lucky, you know that? That you didn't have to wait your whole life to do something special.

Walt, appearing in a flashback, to speak to Jesse,
El Camino: A Breaking Bad Movie (2019).

Yo, yo, yo, 148-3 to the 3 to the 6 to the 9. Representin' the ABQ, what up biatch?! Leave it at the tone.

Jesse's answering machine message when Skyler dials him, "Cat's in the Bag", Season 1.

Have you heard of a company called Gray Matter? Well, I cofounded it in grad school with a couple of friends. Actually, I was the one who named it. And back then, it just, oh, small time. We had a couple of patents pending, but nothing earth-shattering… Care to guess what that company is worth now? Billions. With a B.

Walt tells Jesse (finally) of his Gray Matter company, "Dead Freight", Season 5.

Breaking & Entering 10

"I pitched to AMC that this was going to be a show where we were going to take Mr Chips – mild-mannered schoolteacher Mr White – and we're going to transform him into Scarface."

Vince Gilligan, on his initial pitch of the show to its network AMC, interview with J.C. Freñán, *Slant*, March 29, 2010.

There is gold in the streets just waiting for someone to come and scoop it up.

Walt, to Saul, talking metaphorically about meth, "Madrigal", Season 5.

CHAPTER

3

PSYCHOLOGY

Walter White's descent into drug tyranny exposes
the paradoxes at the core of his Heisenberg
principles: the more he tries to help his family,
the more he ultimately destroys them. Let's take
a bliss-filled hit of Heisenberg and dive down
deep into that badass brain of his and wonder at
what and who, he really was… and why.

I am not in danger, Skyler. I am the danger! A guy opens his door and gets shot and you think that of me? No. I am the one who knocks!

Walt, with the show's most iconic line, "Cornered", Season 4.

We keep hearing a name. Heisenberg. Lately pretty much every dimebagger we come across. Maybe it's a tweaker urban legend. Still, somebody somewhere is cooking that big blue we keep finding.

Hank, on the growing legend of Heisenberg, "Breakage", Season 2.

Breaking & Entering

"We needed an actor to play a character who was very dark and nasty but at the end of the hour you had to feel sorry for him. Bryan Cranston just nailed it."

Vince Gilligan, on finding his Walt in Bryan Cranston, interview with Jon Plunkett, *Guardian*, August 18, 2013.

I did it for me. I liked it.
I was good at it. And… I was…
really… I was alive.

Walt, to Elliott and Gretchen, revealing his motivations
behind transforming into Heisenberg, "Felina", Season 5.

You could have shut your mouth, cooked, and made as much money as you ever needed! It was perfect! But no! You just had to blow it up! You, and your pride and your ego! You just had to be the man!

Mike uses his dying breath to give Walt an ego check, "Say My Name", Season 5.

I can't speak for this Heisenberg that people refer to, but whatever he became, the sweet, kind, brilliant man that we once knew, long ago, he's gone.

Gretchen's last words about her former friend Walt, "Granite State", Season 5.

You know, you never believed in me… You're always whining and complaining about how I make my money, just dragging me down. While I do everything. And now you tell my son what I do after I've told you and told you to keep your goddamn mouth shut. You stupid bitch. How dare you?

Walt's turn to the dark side is complete as he rages with Skyler for the final time, "To'hajiilee", Season 5.

All the people that we've killed — Gale… and the rest. If you believe that there's a hell — I don't know if you're into that — but we're already pretty much going there, right? But I'm not gonna lie down until I get there.

Walt isn't taking his current predicament lying down, "Say My Name", Season 5.

Breaking & Entering 12

"There was such apprehension coming up to knowing, 'It's the last day! The last scene! The last setup! The last take!' You're just like, 'Ugghhh!!! No!!!'
You didn't want it to end."

Bryan Cranston, on the final iconic episode, interview with Dan Snierson, *Entertainment Weekly*, September 28, 2018.

Open your eyes! Can't you see that I needed you on my side to kill Gus?! I ran over those gangbangers! I killed Emilio and Krazy-8! Why? I did all of those things to try to save your life as much as mine, only you're too stupid to know it!

Walt tries to manipulate Jesse to get him back on side, "To'hajiilee", Season 5.

You two guys are just guys. Mr White, he's the devil. He's smarter than you, he's luckier than you. Whatever is supposed to happen, the exact opposite is going to happen.

Jesse tells Gomez and Hank that their plan to catch Walt won't work, "Rabid Dog", Season 5.

Shut the fuck up and let me die in peace.

Mike, mortally wounded (by Walt), bids his killer goodbye for the final time, "Say My Name", Season 5.

There is more money here than we could spend in ten lifetimes. I certainly can't launder it, not with 100 car washes. Please tell me… how much is enough? How big does this pile have to be?

Skyler and Walt assess the family fortune locked up in storage, "Gliding Over All", Season 5.

Breaking Bad: By the Numbers #3

270

The best-guessed body count of how many people were killed as a response to Walt's actions throughout the show's entire run. From the victims aboard Wayfarer 515 to the people executed personally at the hands of Heisenberg, carbon-based lifeforms became nothing more than collateral damage in Walt's empire-building god complex. Can you work out the math?

I built this. Me. Me alone. Nobody else!

Walt, or rather Heisenberg, talks to Skyler about his $80 million drug empire, "To'hajiilee", Season 5.

I know you despise me and I know how much you want to see me dead. But I'm willing to bet there's a man that you hate even more. I'm offering you an opportunity for revenge.

Walt to Hector Salamanca, as events with Gus come to a head, "Face Off", Season 4.

All right, $16,000 laundered at 75 cents on the dollar, minus my fee, which is 17 per cent, comes out to $9,960. Congratulations, you've just left your family a second-hand Subaru.

Saul calculates the profits from the first money laundering, "4 Days Out", Season 2.

Breaking & Entering 13

"I remember reading things: 'Shame on AMC for greenlighting a show that's glamorizing the cooking and selling of meth.' All of that quickly went away the moment we hit the air."

Aaron Paul, on the show's problematic core theme, interview with Dan Snierson, *Entertainment Weekly*, September 28, 2018.

Fuck you and your eyebrows.

Walt tells Bogdan, the car wash owner, where to go, "Pilot", Season 1.

I alone should suffer the consequences of those choices, no one else. And those consequences... they're coming. No more prolonging the inevitable.

Walt and Skyler pack up and prepare to leave in a hurry once it's clear to Walt that Gus is out for his family's blood, "End Times", Season 4.

I'm sorry, after everything you've done for me? What you've done for me?! You've killed me is what you've done! You signed my death warrant! And now you want advice? Alright, I'll give you advice: go to Mexico and screw up like I know you will and wind up in a barrel somewhere!

Walt rejects Jesse's plea to be taught how to cook the blue for the cartel with a thrilling dismissal, "Bug", Season 4.

You mark my words, Skyler.
Toe the line, or you will wind up
just like Hank.

Walt threatens Skyler, "To'hajiilee", Season 5.

Listen, Walter. Just because you shot Jesse James, don't make you Jesse James.

Mike gives Walt an ego check, "Hazard Pay", Season 5.

Breaking & Entering

14

"I knew that *Breaking Bad* could never be a complete success unless it looked not just like a movie, but a great movie. It had to be cinematic with every frame. I wanted it to look like *The Godfather*, I wanted it to look like a John Ford western. We were really shooting for the stars."

Vince Gilligan, on the show's cinematic aesthetic, interview with Emma Dibdin, *Esquire*, January 16, 2018.

We've come this far for us, what's one more?

Skyler, to Walt, about killing off Jesse, "Rabid Dog", Season 5.

Nursing home full of old folks just whet your appetite, now you want to kill a bunch of cops?

Mike quips about Walt's bombing of Casa Tranquila, where Hector lived after his stroke, "Live Free or Die", Season 5.

Look, the day I go in with this, it's the last day of my career, Marie. I'm going to have to walk in there, look those people in the eye and admit that the person I've been chasing the past year is my own brother-in-law.

Hank's days as a loudmouth cop are as he confides to Marie his plan to catch Walt, "Buried", Season 5.

It was you. All along, it was you! You son of a bitch. You drove me into traffic to keep me from that laundry… You bombed a nursing home. Heisenberg! You lying, two-faced sack of shit!

Hank finally meets the real Heisenberg, "Blood Money", Season 5.

If that's true — if you don't know who I am — then maybe your best course would be to tread lightly.

Walt invites Hank to think carefully before making his next move, "Blood Money", Season 5.

You all know exactly who I am. Say my name… I'm the cook. I'm the man who killed Gus Fring… Now say my name.*

Walt insists that competitor Declan refers to him by his true identity, "Say My Name", Season 5.

Upon Declan muttering, "You're Heisenberg", Walter replies, smiling, "You're goddamn right."

Just a couple of days ago, you told me that a man held a gun to your head. You said it like it was a point of pride. There's nothing you can say that'll convince me there won't come a day that somebody will come knocking on that door looking to harm you or me or all of us.

Skyler's plea to Walt to keep Junior and Holly out of harm's reach, "Dead Freight", Season 5.

You are trouble. I'm sorry the kid doesn't see it, but I sure as hell do. You are a time bomb, tick-tick-ticking. And I have no intention of being around for the boom.

Mike gives Walt a dose of reality, "Madrigal", Season 5.

You're not Clarence Darrow, Saul.
You're a two-bit, bus-bench lawyer.
And you work for me. We're done
when I say we're done.

Walt refuses Saul's desire to be done, "Live Free or Die",
Season 5.

Breaking & Entering

"Before this show, I was at the lowest point in my career. I'd been working pretty steadily and I'd have dry spells, I'd get a random commercial that would help me pay rent for a few months. When *Breaking Bad* came to me, I'd kind of run out of money."

Aaron Paul, on Jesse Pinkman transforming his life, interview with Emma Dibdin, *Esquire*, January 16, 2018.

Why am I the only person capable of behaving in a professional manner?

Walt, to Saul, bitching about Jesse, Gus and Mike not behaving in a business-like way, "Bullet Points", Season 4.

Where do I go to make an RV disappear? I'm not David Copperfield!

Walt may share the same name as Disney but he lacks that magic touch, "Sunset", Season 3.

I mean really, what'd you expect me to do? Just simply roll over and allow you to murder us? That I wouldn't take measures — extreme measures — to defend myself? Wrong! Think again.

Walt educates Gus on who he really is, "Box Cutter", Season 4.

This money, I didn't steal it.
It doesn't belong to anyone else.
I earned it. The things I've
done to earn it… the things I've
had to do… I've got to live
with them.

Walt defends his money-orientated motivations to an
increasingly unconvinced Skyler, "I.F.T.", Season 3.

CHAPTER

4

CRIMINOLOGY

Drug deals. Bad guys. Corpse disposals. Fried chicken. Coin flips. *Breaking Bad* had them all and more. With a collection of the most awesome villains in TV history, the show dug down deep into the dark side of society's most dangerous.

Ready to take a sneak-peek into the criminal underworld of New Mexico and Walt's meth empire? Good, because Gus, Tuco, Hector, Eladio, Krazy-8, Welker and Saul are all waiting for you…

This is the guy you want. This is the guy I'd hire. Dude's like Houdini. Seriously, when the going gets tough, you don't want a criminal lawyer, all right? You want a *criminal* lawyer.

Jesse introduces Saul Goodman to Walt,
"Better Call Saul", Season 2.

We tried to poison you because you are an insane, degenerate piece of filth and you deserve to die.

Walt, to Tuco, before Jesse bashes Tuco in the face with a rock and Walt shoots him in the gut, "Grilled", Season 2.

The DEA took all your money, your lab. You got nothing. Square one. But you know the business. And I know the chemistry. I'm thinking… maybe you and I could partner up.

Walt manipulates Jesse (for the first time) into becoming partners, "Pilot", Season 1.

I got two dudes that turned into raspberry slushie then flushed down my toilet. I can't even take a proper dump in there.

Jesse reminisces about Emilio and Krazy-8's death in his house, "A No Rough Stuff Type of Deal", Season 1.

Breaking & Entering 16

"Bryan is the whole package; he's such a fine actor that even if he were the world's biggest asshole, he'd be worth working with."

Vince Gilligan, on Bryan Cranston, interview with Emma Dibdin, *Esquire*, January 16, 2018.

That's what the kids call epic fail.

Saul's perfect response to Walt's idea of hiring a hitman, "Problem Dog", Season 4.

What good is it
being an outlaw if you have
responsibilities?

Jesse learns a lesson about maturity, "Kafkaesque",
Season 3.

Don Eladio is dead. His capos are dead. You have no one left to fight for. Fill your pockets and leave in peace. Or fight me and die!

Gus, near dead from poisoned tequila, bluffs his way out of certain death, "Salud", Season 4.

Breaking & Entering

"Breaking Bad was one of the first series people binge-watched, because the first three seasons all plopped onto Netflix at once. AMC made their deal with Netflix when we were still shooting Season Four, I believe, and that's really when the wave started."

Aaron Paul, on Netflix saving the show's bacon, interview with Emma Dibdin, *Esquire*, January 16, 2018.

Hey, I'm a civilian. I'm not your lawyer anymore. I'm nobody's lawyer. The fun's over. From here on out, I'm Mr Low Profile, just another douchebag with a job and three pairs of Dockers. If I'm lucky, a month from now — best case scenario — I'm managing a Cinnabon in Omaha.

Saul, to Walt, en route to Omaha to find a new line of work, "Granite State", Season 5.

I'm sorry to say, kid, but you're still gonna be two miracles short of sainthood.

Saul, to Jesse, regarding Jesse's plans to take care of Mike's granddaughter, Kaylee, "Blood Money", Season 5.

Breaking Bad: By the Numbers #4

Between Season 4 and the finale of Season 5, the show's audience had grown from 2 million viewers to…

10 million

… a direct result of the first three seasons' popularity on Netflix.

Jesus, Walt, the news here. Gus Fring is dead. He was blown up along with some person from some Mexican cartel and the DEA has no idea what to make of it. Do you know about this? Walt? Was this you?*

Skyler, to Walt, upon hearing the news of Gus's death, killed in Hector's suicide bomb, "Face Off", Season 4.

* Walt's simple response to his wife: "I won."

Breaking & Entering 18

"*Breaking Bad* doesn't engage you passively. It's not a show where you can go cook dinner or mix a drink while it's on. You have to be attentive, because your loyalties to these characters are constantly being tested, and that's where allegiances start to form. It was a show where we were constantly testing the audience to see how far they'll go."

Bryan Cranston, on consistently testing the viewer's allegiances to its central characters, interview with Emma Dibdin, *Esquire*, January 16, 2018.

The agent's name is
Hank Schrader. May his death
satisfy you.

Gus invites Marco to find pleasure in locating Hank,
"Sunset", Season 3.

You two want to go stick your wangs in a hornet's nest, it's a free country. But how come I always gotta get sloppy seconds?

Saul, after hearing of Jesse and Walt's latest cunning plan, "Face Off", Season 4.

Oh, hey, nerdiest old dude I know, you wanna come cook crystal?

Jesse mocks Walt for wanting to cook meth, "Cat's in the Bag" Season 1.

Breaking & Entering

19

"I had specific ways to get out of character at the end of a day. I would wrap a moist towel around my bald head, and another one around my face, and sit there in the makeup and hair trailer and just allow the day's grime and negative energy to escape. I'd wipe it all off of me, and that helped relieve the burden of carrying around this man's darkness."

Bryan Cranston, on throwing off the "heavy overcoat" of Walt's ego after a day's shoot, interview with Emma Dibdin, *Esquire*, January 16, 2018.

So, what? Is this going to be a regular thing now? Meth cooking and corpse disposal?

Walt sums up the show's recent events in a nutshell after a sniper victim's body ends up at the superlab, "Bug", Season 4.

You are not the guy. You're not capable of being the guy.
I had a guy but now I don't. You are not the guy.

Mike, to Jesse, who's not the guy Mike needs,
"Shotgun", Season 4.

You want me to beg? You're the smartest guy I ever met. And you're too stupid to see… he made up his mind ten minutes ago. Do what you're gonna do—

Hank refuses to beg for his life before Jack Welker pulls the trigger, "To'hajiilee", Season 5.

Clearly Walt's taste in women is the same as his taste in lawyers: only the very best with just the right amount of dirty.

Saul makes the best kind of worst first impression when meeting Skyler, "Abiquiu", Season 3.

Any other drugs in the house? Think hard. Your freedom depends on it. Here's your story: you woke up. You found her. That's all you know. Say it.

Mike slaps Jesse into shape after the death of Jane, "ABQ", Season 2.

If you want to stay a criminal and not become a convict then maybe you should grow up and listen to your lawyer.

Saul tells Jesse about the IRS, "Kafkaesque", Season 3.

Breaking & Entering 20

"I was out for dinner last night, and someone just came right up to me screaming, 'Science, bitch!' I get called 'bitch' every single day. I have been called 'bitch' more than anyone on the planet, and that is very exciting. I'm very proud of that fact."

Aaron Paul, on Jesse's infamous catchphrase, interview with Emma Dibdin, *Esquire*, January 16, 2018.

I hide in plain sight, same as you. Are we done?

Gus sees his mirrored reflection in Walt, "I See You", Season 3.

Walter, I'm your lawyer. Anything you say to me is totally privileged. I'm not in the shakedown racket. I'm a lawyer. Even drug dealers need lawyers, right? Especially drug dealers.

Saul's not in the shakedown racket apparently, "Better Call Saul", Season 2.

I think he just lacks the proper... motivation.*

Skyler, on Bogdan's refusal to sell the car wash to Walt and Skyler, "Open House", Season 4.

Or, as Saul calls it — "Attitude adjustment."

I assure you I could kill you from way over here if it makes you feel any better.

Mike reassures Walt that he's dangerous no matter the distance between them, "Full Measure", Season 3.

You are a wealthy man now, and one must learn to be rich. To be poor, anyone can manage.

Gus educates Walt about the problems of having too much money, "Abiquiu", Season 3.

The moral of the story is, I chose a half measure when I should have gone all the way. I'll never make that mistake again. No more half measures, Walter.

Mike tells Walt the story of the big boy and the little bird, "Half Measures", Season 3.

I am not turning down the money!
I'm turning down you! You get it?!
I want nothing to do with you! Ever since
I met you, everything I ever cared about
is gone! Ruined, turned to shit,
dead, ever since I hooked up with 'the
great Heisenberg'! I have never been
more alone!

Jesse turns Walter down for the $3 million cook —
or does he?, "Sunset", Season 3.

I'm here because I owe you the courtesy and respect to tell you this personally. I'm done. It has nothing to do with you personally. I find you extraordinarily professional, and I appreciate the way you do business. I'm just… making a change in my life is what it is, and I'm at something of a crossroads… and it's brought me to a realization: I am not a criminal. No offense to any people who are, but… this is not me.

Walt turning down Gus Fring's $3 million that might turn out to be too good to refuse, "No Más", Season 3.

She's not going to the cops, she's not telling a living soul. You wanna know why? One word: blowback. If she blabs, it'll be a disaster – for her.

Saul comforts Walt with legal advice that Skyler's not a threat, "Caballo sin Nombre", Season 3.

If you want to make more money and keep the money that you make – Better Call Saul!

Saul's advice to Walt and Jesse, "Better Call Saul", Season 2.

What do I look like, Scarface?

Jesse, to Walt, who may have the wrong idea of Jesse's drug dealer status, "Crazy Handful of Nothin'", Season 1.

CHAPTER

5

METHODOLOGY

At the centre of all *Breaking Bad*'s plotting was Walt and Jesse's blue sky meth, glass so pure it made those who touched it impure to the core, shattering their lives into a million shards. But *Breaking Bad*, at its core, is so much more than the misadventures of meth-peddling; it is the methodological and microscopic study of how carbon-based lifeforms behave under volatile stress. Meth was just a metaphor for greed, envy and desire.

For our final hit, let's lay back and relax and bathe in the enduring legacy of some of TV's greatest lines about meth, mayhem and mild-mannered maniacs. Not to be snorted at.

Put me on your magical boat, man, and sail me down your chocolatey river of meth!

Badger, Jesse's junkie friend, equates Jesse with Willy Wonka (another W.W.), "Bit By a Dead Bee", Season 2.

Come on, man, some straight like you, giant stick up his ass, all of a sudden at age what, 60, he's just gonna break bad?

Jesse, to Walt (aged 50), questioning his motivations to break bad, "Pilot", Season 1.

Breaking & Entering 21

"We informed the DEA – with all due respect and consideration – that we're doing this show, and 'Would you like to be a part of it in a consultancy in order to make sure that we get it right?' They had the choice to say, 'We don't want anything to do with it.' But they saw that it might be in their best interest to make sure that we do it correctly. So DEA chemists came onboard as consultants and taught Aaron Paul and me how to make crystal meth."

Bryan Cranston, on consulting with the DEA while filming, interview with Emma Dibdin, *Esquire*, January 16, 2018.

Yours is just some tepid, off-brand, generic cola. What I'm making is Classic Coke… Do you really want to live in a world without Coca-Cola?

Walt, to his Phoenix-based competitor, Declan, "Say My Name", Season 5.

Breaking Bad: By the Numbers #5

$82 million

The total amount revealed as Walter White's earnings during the two-year duration of *Breaking Bad's* timeline, starting, of course, on Walt's 50th birthday.

This kicks like a mule with its balls wrapped in duct tape!

Tuco Salamanca approves of Walt and Jesse's cook, "Crazy Handful of Nothin", Season 1.

It may be blue, but it's the bomb!

Jesse brags to Tuco about blue sky's purity,
"A No-Rough-Stuff-Type Deal", Season 1.

Partners in what? What exactly do you do here, I've been meaning to ask. I cook. But from what I can tell, you are just a drug addict! You are a pathetic junkie too stupid to understand and follow simple rudimentary instructions!

Walt gets real with Jesse at the height of his junk addiction, "Down", Season 2.

Look, let's start with some tough love, alright? Ready for this? Here it goes: you two suck at peddling meth.

Saul speaks wisdom to Walt and Jesse after some backward steps, "Mandala", Season 2.

It's methamphetamine.
But I'm a manufacturer, I'm
not a dealer.

Walt confesses , for the first time, to Skyler his
extracurricular activities, "No Más", Season 3.

Blue, yellow, pink, whatever, man! Just keep bringing me that!

Tuco gets excited about Walt and Jesse's pure blue sky product, "A No-Rough-Stuff-Type Deal", Season 1.

Breaking & Entering

22

Walter White's drug kingpin alter ego, Heisenberg, is a name borrowed from Werner Heisenberg (1901–1976), a Nobel Prize-winning physicist who developed the principle of uncertainty and was famed for his quote…

"Not only is the Universe stranger than we think, it is stranger than we can think. What we observe is not nature itself, but nature exposed to our method of questioning."

Let me get this straight, Russell. You got this meth from 'some dude' wearing khaki pants, who — you're 80 per cent sure — had a moustache. And that's it? That's your brain working at full capacity?

Hank interrogates Russell in the only way he knows how, "Green Light", Season 3.

Did you know that there's an acceptable
level of rat turds that can go into candy
bars? It's the government, jack. Even
government doesn't care that much
about quality. You know what is okay to
put in hot dogs? Pig lips and assholes.
But I say, 'Hey, have at it bitches,'
'cause I love hot dogs.

Jesse isn't so fussed about quality control, "Fly", Season 3.

Yo! Gatorade me, bitch!

Jesse's most famous bitch-related line, "Fly", Season 3.

You and I both forget about Pinkman. We forget this ever happened. We consider this a lone hiccup in an otherwise long and fruitful business arrangement. I prefer option B.

Walt tells Gus his options after the double cross, "Full Measure", Season 3.

I trust the hole in the desert I'd leave you in.

Mike's one-liners come thick and fast while on the hunt for Jesse, "Full Measure", Season 3.

If I can't kill you, you'll sure as shit wish you were dead.

Jesse, to Walt, about Gus, after watching him execute Victor, "Box Cutter", Season 4.

For what it's worth, getting the shit kicked out of you? Not to say you get used to it, but you do kinda get used to it.

Jesse, on getting used to getting the shit kicked out of him, "Open House", Season 4.

Hey, nobody appreciates a passionate woman more than I do, but in this business — and Walt can back me up on this — the number one rule is, 'Don't take things personal.'

Saul, on the arrival of Skyler into Walt's business empire, "Open House", Season 4.

Breaking & Entering 23

The show's title card and the prominent colour scheme of Walt's clothing is green, despite blue being the most mentioned colour, and the colour of the meth that Walt cooks. This is because the show's creator, Vince Gilligan, wanted to represent Walt's greed for money and growth and envy, through its most associated colour - green.

He was a meth chef. We're talking five stars, candles and white tablecloth, y'know. I can't believe these words are coming out of my mouth, but he was a genius, plain and simple. I mean, uh, boy, if he applied that big brain of his to something good, I dunno, who knows? He could've helped humanity or something like that.

Hank, ruffling Walt's feathers with talk of Gale's genius, "Shotgun", Season 4.

Gustavo Fring, blue meth…
Whole thing is off-the-map nuts.
I ought to be wearing a tinfoil
hat, you know?

Hank tries to correlate the strange connection between
fried chicken and Walt's brand of poison,
"Problem Dog", Season 4.

Breaking Bad: By the Numbers #6

99.1%*

The purity of Walt and Jesse's blue sky meth.

* Interestingly, Forbes reported that the purity of meth on U.S. streets has increased from 39 per cent purity in 2008 (when the show started) to more than 93 per cent purity in 2018.

So, what if this is like math or algebra? Add a plus douchebag to a minus douchebag, and you get, like, zero douchebags?

Jesse's math about Hank being on to Gus doesn't add up to Walt*, "Hermanos", Season 4.

* Walt retorts: "I've got some math for you: Hank catching Gus equals Hank catching us!"

A guy this clean's gotta be dirty.

Hank's tracking of Gus's movements prove complicated, "Bug", Season 4.

Mr White, look, I need your help.
OK, maybe you could like coach me
or something, or you could give me
some notes. Mr White?

Jesse pleads with Walt to teach him how to cook the blue
after Gus forces Jesse to cook with the cartel chemists
in Mexico, "Bug", Season 4.

I get it, the guy is a complete and total dick, but if something… final… happens to Mr. White, we're going to have a problem.

Jesse protects his partner against Gus's "appropriate response" to Walt's actions, "End Times", Season 4.

Breaking & Entering

24

INT. WINNEBAGO — DAY

Inside, the DRIVER's knuckles cling white to the wheel. He's got the pedal flat. Scared, breathing fast. His eyes bug wide behind the faceplate of his gas mask.

Oh, by the way, he's wearing a GAS MASK. That, and white jockey UNDERPANTS. Nothing else.

The first introduction to Walt inside the RV in the pilot episode's script, written by Vince Gilligan.

Yeah, yeah, stop showing off for the client, Honey Tits!

Saul calls assistant Francesca "H.T." for the last time, much to her objection, "End Times", Season 4.

If you're committed enough, you
can make any story work.
I once convinced a woman I was
Kevin Costner, and it worked,
because I believed it!

Saul, on becoming Kevin Costner, "Abiquiu" Season 3.

Christ. You two. All I can say is if I ever get anal polyps, I'll know what to name them.

Saul's classic quip breaks the tension with a highly-strung Jesse, "Face Off", Season 4.

Where'd you get your law degree, Goodman? The same clown college you got that suit?

Hank visits Saul for a vis-à-vis chat about his recent shenanigans, "Dead Freight", Season 5.

It's like Scarface had sex with Mr Rogers or something.

Hank, about poor dead Gale, "Shotgun", Season 4.

You listen to me, bitch. You get your ass out here as fast as you can. And don't even think about calling anyone for help. You hang up on me, put me on hold, lose my call for any reason — as soon as you do — I'm burning all of it. Fire in the hole, bitch.

Jesse threatens to burn all of Walt's money after teaming up with Hank, "Buried", Season 5.

Say the words. Say you want this. Nothing happens until I hear you say it.

Jesse's final exchange with Walt ends with Jesse driving off in his El Camino – the most wanted man in America, "Felina", Season 5.

Everyone sounds like
Meryl Streep with a gun to
their head.

Mike, about Lydia, as Walt and Jesse discuss
killing her off, "Dead Freight", Season 5.

Well, they're here. The end times, kid. End times.

Saul tells Jesse the end is nigh after Gus threatens a bolting Walt and his family, "End Times", Season 4.

It's Walt. How are you feeling? Kind of under the weather? Like you've got the flu? That would be the ricin I gave you. I slipped it into that stevia crap that you're always putting in your tea. Well... goodbye, Lydia.

Walt utters his immortal last lines to a poisoned Lydia, "Felina", Season 5.